Sammy Learns To Read At 3

Dedicated To

The next generation of change agents and the parents and educators responsible to nurture them.

Given the right teachings and guidance, the children of today can pave the path to a brighter tomorrow.

Sammy Learns To Read At 3

By

Samuel Browne

SAMMY LEARNS TO READ AT 3

Sammy Learns To Read At 3
by
Samuel Browne

All rights reserved, including the right to reproduce this book or portions thereof in any for whatsoever

Published by NGOWE
www.ngowe.com
Tampa Fl, 33611

Copyright 2016 Samuel Browne

1st Edition: 2016

ISBN
978-0998320427

Illustrated by
Bassey Inyang
Charles Casper

ACKNOWLEDGEMENTS

The writer wishes to thank God for blessing him with wonderful parents, good mentors and role models in his life. He was born in 1999 when Governor Zell Miller and former teacher introduced a CD of classical music to all new mothers. The Governor's initiative stemmed from research showing a link between listening to classical music and enhanced brain development in infants and its ability to improve mathematical and logic skills in older children. This CD was used as a lullaby during naptime every day and was especially important when his sister Daniella was born. This CD was part of a formula to create early learners, and it did not work alone. We added the following ingredients to the recipe: a holistic lifestyle, creativity, dedication, repetition, commitment and lots of love and kisses.

INTRODUCTION

Sammy Learn To Read At 3 by Samuel Browne is a collaboration with his mother, Valerie Browne. This book is a combination of learning tools and techniques practiced over generations with new exciting concepts added to make the learning experience fun and exciting. A child's mind is like a "little sponge," therefore every minute of his or her development should be a learning experience. Teaching is fun, continuous and should begin when the baby is in the womb. From birth, a child continues to learn, and the first sound made is associated with a letter sound. Learning must be reinforced through games, singing, repetition, memorization, innovation, creativity, and excitement because it lays a good foundation for their future. Samuel wants to be a living example to other youths to show how focus, passion, dedication, and commitment to success can result in achieving one's goals.

Sammy was a curious little boy who loved to run and play but most of all he loves to sing and say his ABC.

"Sammy, we had so much fun learning the ABC, can you remember what you learned?"

"Each letter in the alphabet comes both big and small, and it is fun to know them all. Let us play the Alphabet Guessing Game!!!" Mommy said excitedly.

"Yeh, that sounds fun!!!" Sammy shouted and waited eagerly.

"Big A little a, what begins with A Sammy?"
"Ant!!!" Sammy shouted.

"Big B little b, what begins with B?"
"Ball!"

"Big C little c what begins with C?"
"Car!"

Dd   "Big D little d?"
"Duck!"

Ee   "Big E little e?"
"Egg!"

Ff   "Big F little f?"
"Fish!"

Gg   "Big G little g?"
"Giraffe!"

Hh   "Big H little h?"
"House!"

Ii   "Big I little i?"
"Ink!"

"Big J little j?"
"Jug!"

"Big K little k?"
"Key!"

"Big L little l?"
"Lion!"

"Big M little m?"
"Moon!"

"Big N little n?"
"Net!"

"Big O little o?"
"Ostrich!"

Pp   "Big P little p?" "Pot!"

Qq   "Big Q little q?" "Queen!"

Rr   "Big R little r?" "Rat!"

Ss   "Big S little s?" "Star"

Tt   "Big T little t?" "Toy!"

Uu   "Big U little u?" "Unicorn."

"Big V little v?"
"Van!"

"Big W little w?"
"Water!"

"Big X little x?"
"Xylophone!"

 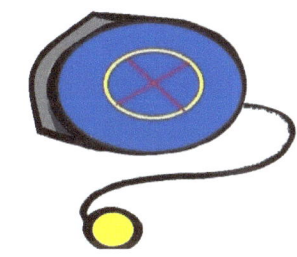

"Big Y little y?"
"Yo-yo!"

"Big Z little z, what begins with z?"

"ZEBRA

I DID IT!!!"

Sammy and Mommy danced, sang, and played for the rest of the day. They had fun with puzzles, alphabet guessing games, and videos about the ABC.

That night

when

Sammy went

to bed

Mommy played

MOZART

in his

head.

The next day

Mommy placed

familiar two letter words

on the wall for him

to practice

some useful

sight words

he needs

to know.

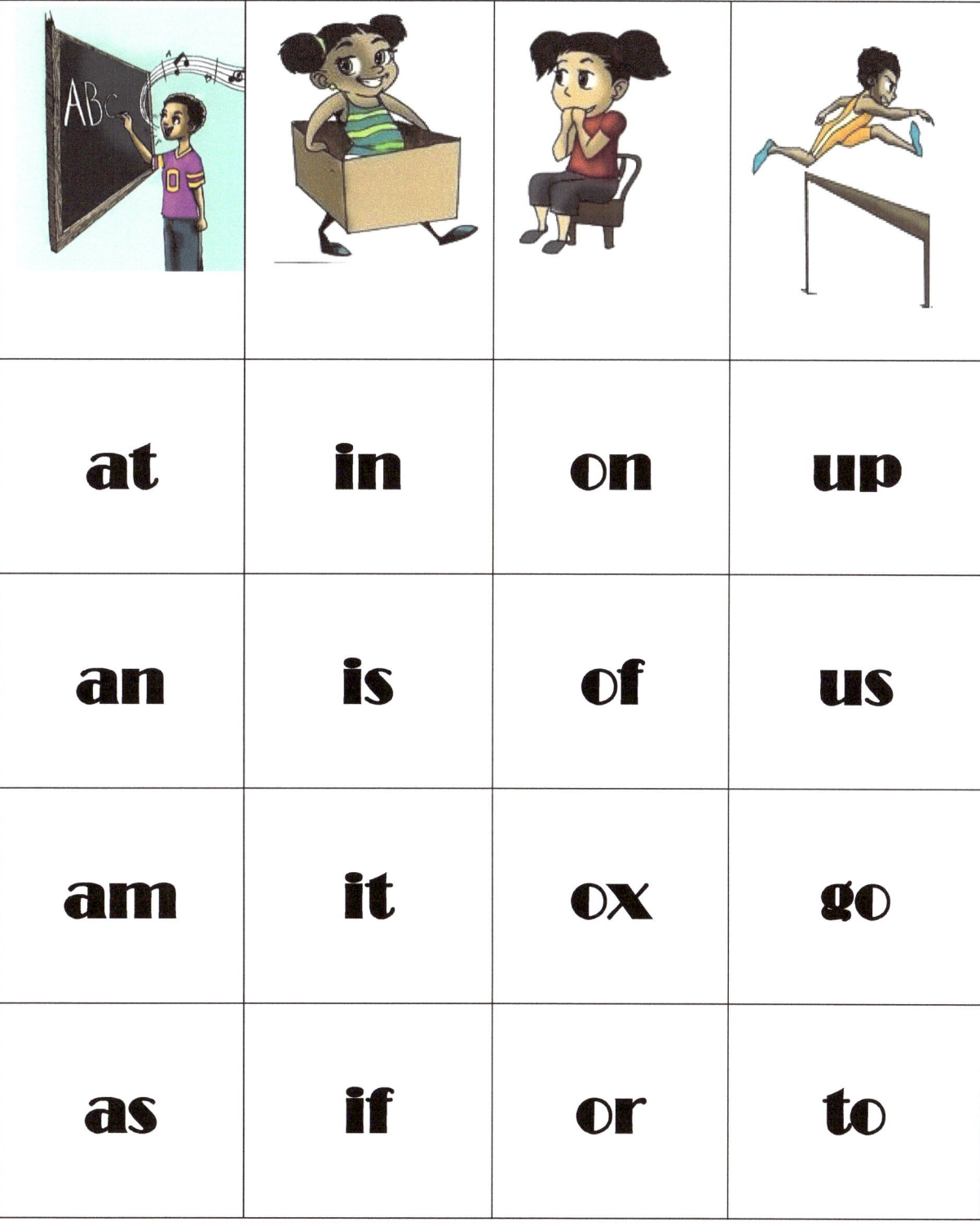

When Sammy woke up, he remembered all his fun words. Mommy took the time to teach him **vowel** sounds because without vowels some words would not sound right.

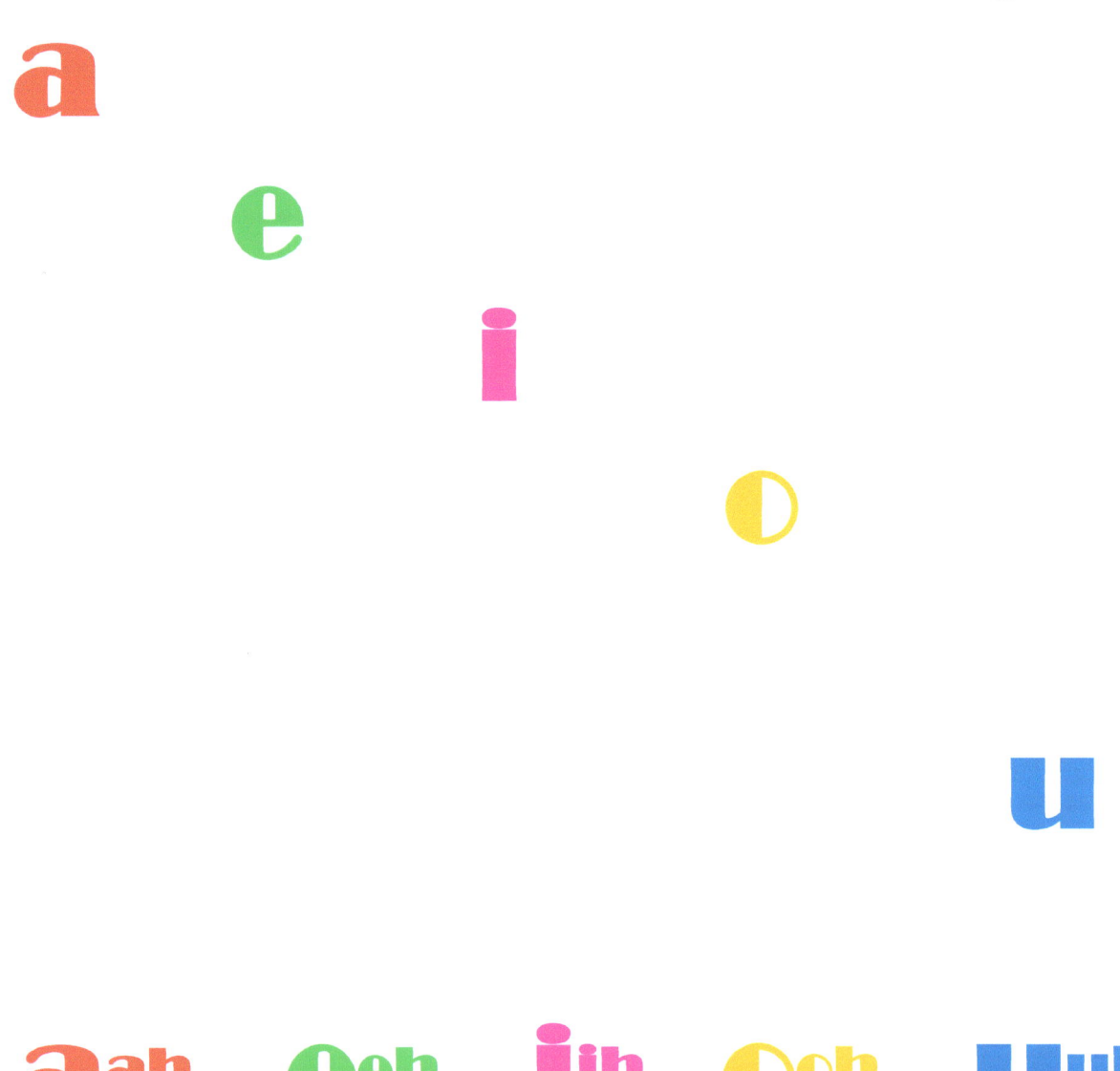

"When you form words with consonants and vowels you learn to read and you get wiser."

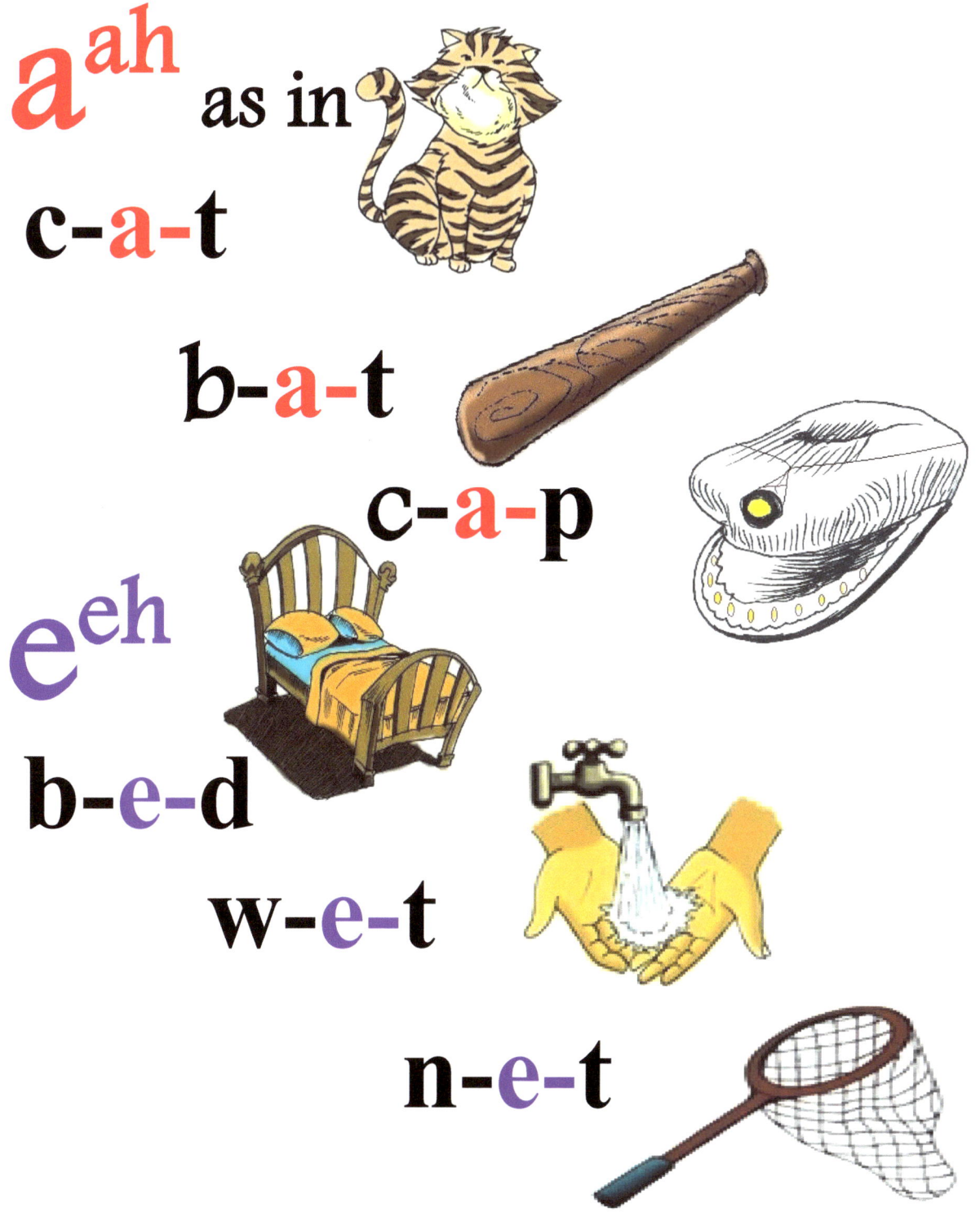

a^{ah} as in

c-a-t

b-a-t

c-a-p

e^{eh}

b-e-d

w-e-t

n-e-t

u^{uh}

c-u-p

s-u-n

h-u-t

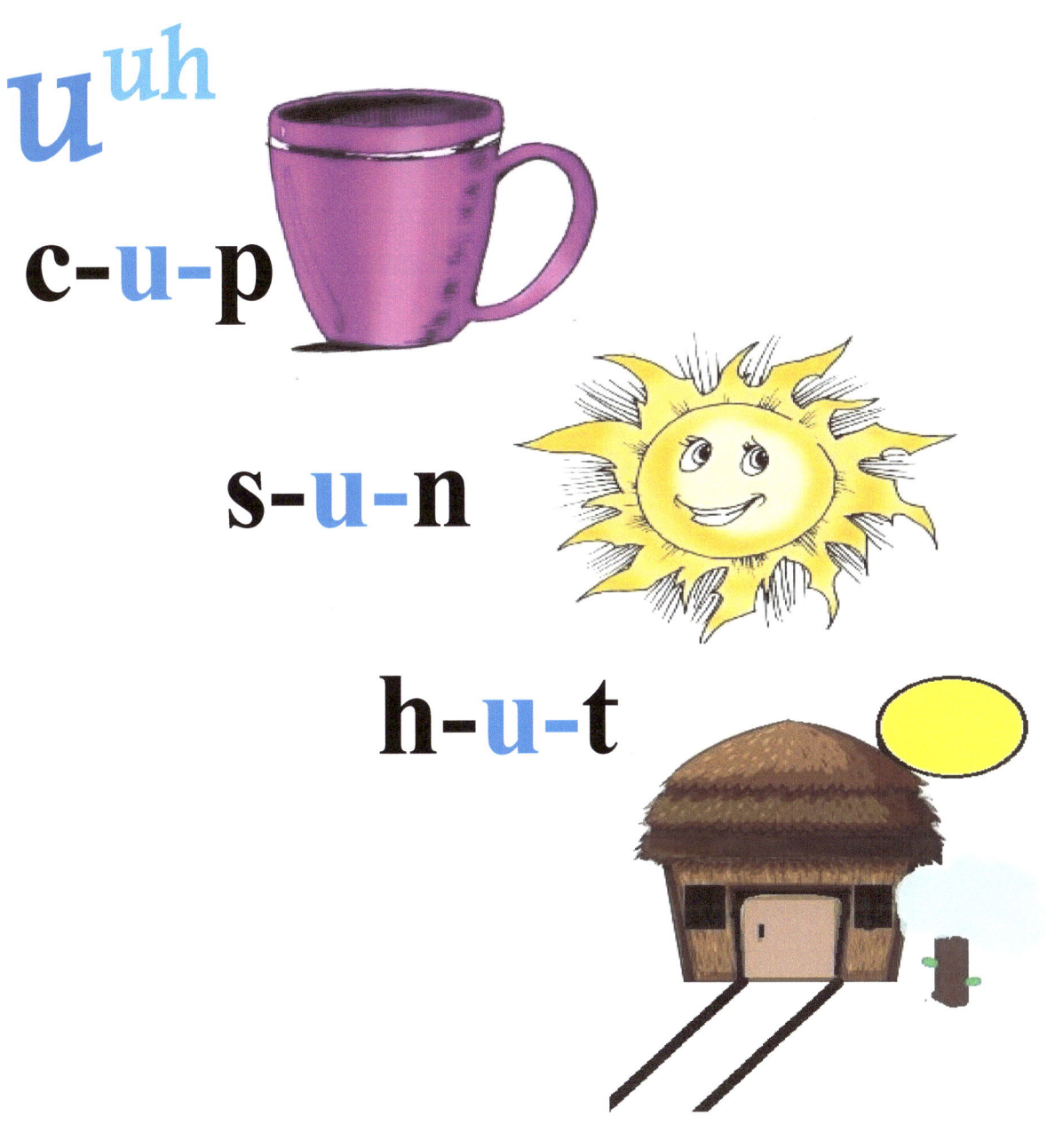

"They are fun and magical too,"
Mommy said mysteriously.

That evening Sammy said, "Mommy I had so much fun sounding words let us play more sounding word games to see what I know."

b-a-t bat	c-a-n can	f-a-n fan	h-a-t hat
j-a-m jam	m-a-d mad	m-a-t mat	y-a-m yam
B-e-n Ben	h-e-n hen	m-e-n men	p-e-n pen
p-e-t pet	r-e-d red	t-e-n ten	v-e-t vet
b-i-g big	d-i-g dig	d-i-p dip	f-i-g fig
p-i-n pin	r-i-b rib	w-i-n win	z-i-p zip
b-o-x box	b-o-y boy	f-o-x fox	h-o-g hog
h-o-t hot	l-o-g log	m-o-p mop	p-o-p pop
b-u-n bun	b-u-s bus	b-u-g bug	c-u-t cut
f-u-n fun	m-u-g mug	r-u-g rug	t-u-b tub

"Sammy, I will tell you what I see; you will sound out the word, and then tell me the letters that the word begins with."

"I see a dog and a cat, what letter do they begin with?" Mom asked.
"D-o-g starts with D and C-a-t is C," Sammy replied.

"I see a man; what letter begins the word man?"
"M-a-n is the letter m."

"Boy begins with?" Mommy asked.
"B-o-y starts with b."

"I see a car?"
"C-a-r begins with c."

"When the letter 'I' stands alone you point to yourself because it sounds like the letter itself."

"I am Sammy."

"Here are some more words you need to know by sight, they are fun and full of might."

he	my
she	see
we	was
they	are
with	were
so	put
no	for
go	from
big	and
have	yes

"Now

let us put together

some fun words

to make easy phrases.

They will show

that you are

becoming smarter

as you grow."

I am

You are

He is

She is

It is

We are

They are

Shopping is lots of fun for Sammy and Mommy, so in the car they went. Sammy sounds out the fun stuff as they go.

"Sammy, look out the window and say what words you can see."
"I see the word c-o-p for cop and c-a-b for cab."

"That sign says s-t-o-p. What word is that Mom?" and mom helps him to pronounce the word stop.

"The street sign spells P-a-m B-a-y and it is Pam Bay, c-a-r for the car, m-a-n for the man, and s-u-n is for the sun in the sky." Sammy said happily.

"What does b-o-o-k spell Mom?
"That word is book, Sammy."

When they got home,

Mommy said to Sammy.

"After you rest

we will play a fun game

by putting words together

to make easy phrases."

Sammy sighed and said,

"Please let us do it right now

because I cannot wait that long."

I am Sam	Sam, I am
I am a boy	In the bed
In the box	By the box
In the mud	In the car
I have a cat	Do you see my cat?
He put his paw on me	We sit and p-l-a-y all day

For dinner,

Sammy sat with his dad

and showed him

all the wonderful words

he learned how to spell

by using the letters

in his alphabet

soup.

That night

when Sammy

went to bed

mommy played

BEETHOVEN

in his

head.

HELPFUL HINTS AND FUN IDEAS

- Make the ABC and numbers some of their favorite songs.
- **Sing the Alphabet Song in** many versions and have fun singing it with different tempos.
- **Play the ABC games** to learn letter sounds.
- **Guess what comes next** – Parent starts off with the letter 'A' and allows the child to guess what comes next.
- **Begin teaching the uppercase letters first** because they are easier to identify and start with the letters in the Childs name.
- **Play with alphabet letters.** Use magnets, blocks, puzzles or whatever you have, name the letters, have the child repeat the sound, and eventually the child will identify the letter names on his or her own.
- **Matching pictures with sounds/words.** Use pictures to match with sounds/words. It helps develop the child's cognitive abilities.
- **Letter scrambles game.** unscramble letters to make the ABC and words.
- **Treasure hunt** – place the alphabet in order on the table. Place toys all over the ground or in hidden places. Allow the child to find the objects and allow them to match the object with the letters on the table.
- **Phonological Awareness** – play word and rhyming games to facilitate understand and manipulation of the spoken language.
- **Use the outdoors as a major learning experience.**
- **Introduce** different languages (like Spanish, French and Hebrew), learn music/musical instruments, dance, or any creative expression.
- Busy moms have to seize every opportunity to create learning moments.

AUTHORS BIOGRAPHY

Samuel Browne was born in 1999 in Atlanta Georgia but grew up on the beautiful island of St. Croix United States Virgin Island and Nigeria, West Africa. He grew up an active child involved in soccer, basketball, baseball, tennis, and track and field. However, soccer was his main passion. He is an amazing soccer player and hopes that one day he is discovered by the national soccer team. He currently attends college and played for the Tampa Bay United U17 Soccer team. At present, his primary interests are education, writing poetry and songs, playing his piano, developing video games, and of course playing soccer. His creativity and passion for life allow him to look deep within himself to write. His ambition in life is to be the best he could be and become an inspiration to others. Learn more about Yasad Samuel Browne at

www.YasadBrowne.com
Website: **www.ngowe.com**
Twitter & Facebook – NGOWE BOOKS

THE SAMMY SERIES:
Sammy Learns His ABC
Sammy Please Wash Your Hands

OTHER BOOKS
Life To Me
The Sketcher
Melissa Against The World

www.ingramcontent.com/pod-product-compliance
Lightning Source LLC
Chambersburg PA
CBHW060758090426
42736CB00002B/80